JOHN F. KENNEDY

A BOOK OF PAINTINGS

JACQUELINE DUHÉME

JOHN F. KENNEDY

A BOOK OF PAINTINGS

New York   1967   ATHENEUM

I HAVE ALWAYS been fascinated by great men—not because they are famous, but because they are great—and I have been privileged in my not-too-long existence to become the friend of artists such as Henri Matisse, Pablo Picasso and Paul Eluard. But political men! Brr. That is quite another story.... Until I saw for the first time John Kennedy with his family on the television screen when they visited Paris in 1961.

I was not the only Parisian to be surprised! I think everyone was absolutely overwhelmed by the radiant charm and the simplicity of Jack and Jackie Kennedy. To us, in France, the image of world politics is something usually a bit more austere.

It has been natural for me ever since the age of three to express all my feelings in drawings, and I immediately proceeded to illustrate on paper my impressions of the Kennedys' visit to Paris. My little doodles were shortly after that reproduced by the French women's magazine, "Elle," and the next thing to happen was a telephone call from Pierre Salinger, in which he said that the Kennedys had seen my drawings and wanted to compliment me. Would I care to visit them in Washington?

To say that I was taken by surprise is to put it lightly; I was even quite intimidated at first (although I am not usually considered a shy girl). Well, I packed my best things and my painting kit, and soon after made my entrance into the White House through the back door. A few minutes later I felt as if I had been a member of the Presidential family for ages.

How could I possibly describe it? The days I spent with the Kennedys in Washington and in Hyannis Port were really wonderful. Such effortless friendliness, such sincere and natural generosity was something quite rare. And who was I? No ambassador, no politically significant person; I was nothing more than a completely unknown and unimportant French girl—and the only experience I had had in common with the Kennedys was those poor little drawings of mine, in which I had tried to express my fondness for their youthful image as best I could.

I may be politically ignorant, but girls, and even French girls, have a natural feeling about certain things. The impression Jack Kennedy gave me, with his relaxed humor, his intelligent good looks, his immediate awareness of every big or trivial thing, was that nothing wrong could come from such a man, even if he made mistakes at times as any human person will do. One felt that he did not need power because he had enough power in himself; one felt that he could be trusted because he had so much energy that he would never be dependent on others, or on a political career, to do what he felt he had to do.

I have never had such a sense of loss as I felt during that terrible day of November 1963. It was too much, too unbearable.... The world had been young again for a few months, and already it was over: all because some jealous, frustrated maniac had wanted to deprive mankind of that clear, wonderful hope. At the same time one felt there was something fatal about that disaster; the little men had made Jack Kennedy pay the price for his genius.

But he has left behind him something that no one will easily forget, and he has at least given us the living proof that our world can one day become a better place for all of us—good or bad, children or adults.

I hope that something of my love and admiration for Jack Kennedy will be conveyed through the nineteen little tableaux with which I have attempted to describe his life. Of course my paintings are meant for children, and if my images appear naïve, as some will say, it is because that is how I see the world. At least they will show the children of America that the legend of Jack Kennedy is very much alive in the heart of the whole world.

May I say also how much I owe to Jacqueline Kennedy, for her friendship and encouragement, and for the example of her great courage.... I also owe her something else; for in the picture of Jack Kennedy's election as Senator I borrowed from her, and interpreted in my style her own illustration of the event—it would have been impossible to do it better than she did.

Jacqueline Duhéme

JOHN F. KENNEDY

A BOOK OF PAINTINGS

"Man can be as big as he wants. No problem of human destiny is beyond human beings. Man's reason and spirit have often solved the seemingly unsolvable—and we believe they can do it again."

JOHN F. KENNEDY
speech at American University—June 10, 1963

LIFE began for John F. Kennedy on May 29, 1917, in a gray shingled house on Beals Street in Brookline, Massachusetts. His father was Joseph P. Kennedy, a man of determination and ambition—the son of a state senator; his mother was Rose Fitzgerald Kennedy, daughter of John F. Fitzgerald, a mayor of Boston. The family was pleased to have a second son, a brother for Joseph Jr., born two years before.

Jack, as John came to be called, and Joe were too close in age not to be competitors, especially in a family where competition was encouraged. Joe was older and stronger, but Jack was seldom willing to let him get too far ahead. Jack stood up for his own, even when he got the worst of it, as he did most of the time. In fact, he not only defended himself vigorously, he sometimes went on the offensive; there was the occasion, for example, when he stole the chocolate icing Joe had saved for last at the side of his plate. When Jack annoyed him, Joe did not hold back his punches. But Jack remained undaunted and ready to try again.

The boys attended Dexter school together, a few blocks from home. Each day they raced to and from school on their bicycles. Competition and the will to win were a part of everything they did. In time they were both on the football team at Dexter. Joe showed superior athletic ability, but Jack did not. What he lacked in natural ability, he made up in determination and reckless courage.

Over the years the Kennedy family grew. Eventually there were five girls and four boys. When Jack was nine they moved from Brookline to New York City, and then when he was twelve to Bronxville, a New York City suburb. But more important than these homes was the summer house Joseph Kennedy bought for his family in Hyannis Port, Massachusetts, the same year he moved the family to Bronxville.

It was at Hyannis Port that Jack came to love the sea. Nothing was as important as swimming and sailing, not even eating. To both Jack and Joe Jr. sailing was an extremely serious undertaking. Anyone who sailed with them had to be aware of how important winning a race was. If one of the younger children wasn't paying attention when his skipper—Joe or Jack—gave an order, he faced being promptly dumped into the water.

Jack went away to the Canterbury School when he was thirteen. That school year was cut short by an appendectomy. And the following year he joined Joe, Jr., at Choate. There Jack read avidly, but only those things he wanted to read. He spent more time with his friends and at sports than he did on his studies. People and activities challenged him in those years more than abstract ideas. He graduated in 1935, 64th in a class of 112; but his classmates voted him "the most likely to succeed."

He entered Harvard a year later. Here, his first two years were much like the years at Choate. Though Joe was a varsity football player and an excellent student, Jack was outstanding only in his capacity for making friends and his determination to make some kind of athlete out of himself.

Then a European tour in 1937, and subsequent trips abroad while his father was serving as the U.S. Ambassador in London, awakened him to the excitement of world politics. As a result, for the first time, he became really involved in his school studies. His senior thesis, *Why England Slept*, was good enough to be published; and he graduated in 1940 with honors in political science.

John Kennedy graduated from college at a time when planning a future was difficult. War seemed inevitable and the armed forces just around the corner for all young men. In 1941 he tried to get into the Army, but failed the physical examination because of a back injury received playing football at Harvard. He tried the Navy next, with the same results. So he put himself through a series of vigorous exercises to strengthen his back. And finally in September 1941 he won a direct commission in the Naval Reserve. After a year in Washington and the South, he was sent to Motor Torpedo Boat training schools in Portsmouth, New Hampshire, and Melville, Rhode Island. Early in 1943, he was placed in command of PT 109, with a crew of ten men and two other officers. It was just what he wanted.

PT 109 was part of a squadron of PT boats in operation near Guadalcanal in the Solomon Islands. Under Kennedy, it carried out thirty attacks and strafing missions against Japanese ships and shore installations and was on the thirty-first on the night of August 2, 1943. PT 109 was the lead ship of three American PT boats searching for the enemy. It was 2:30 AM, a black, still night. Lt. (j.g.) Kennedy was at the wheel when suddenly a black, hulking shape materialized out of the dark. A Japanese destroyer was headed directly for the 109. Before any action could be taken, the destroyer crashed into the small, wooden-hulled PT boat, slicing it in two.

Hardly noticing the devastated PT boat, the destroyer continued on its course. Kennedy found himself in dangerous waters far from help. Two men did not respond to his call for survivors, but ten others did, all badly shaken. One of the men, Patrick McMahon, had been severely burned. Another had an injured leg.

The men waited for help, but none came. The PT 109 had been given up for lost by its companions. Finally Kennedy directed his men to swim to an island three and a half miles away. Although his back had been reinjured in the collision, there was no time to think of that. Taking the strap of McMahon's life belt between his teeth, Kennedy set off for the island, towing the burned man along. His years of swimming practice stood him in good stead, and he reached the island before any of the other men arrived.

For the next two days, with only brief rest periods, Kennedy with the help of those men who were able, swam and paddled a dug-out canoe around the area, looking for food and help. Finally some friendly natives appeared in camp. Kennedy scratched a message on a coconut shell and entrusted it to the natives, hoping they would deliver it into the right hands. They did, and he and his crew were finally rescued. He was decorated with the Navy and Marine Corps Medal for his efforts.

After his rescue, Kennedy could have returned to the United States, but he requested a second tour of duty on PT boats in the South Pacific. During this time he constantly irritated his reinjured back and also contracted malaria. When he did return to the United States as a PT Boat instructor at Miami, Florida, he was tired and thin.

In the spring of 1944, he had to have an operation on his spine. While he was recuperating, he learned that his brother Joe had been killed. Joe had been a Navy pilot in Europe and had died flying a plane loaded with high explosives over a German rocket base.

The death of Joe shocked and saddened the whole Kennedy family. Often Joe had spoken of going into politics—it was the family tradition. Now he was gone, and John was the oldest son.

For a while after he got out of the Navy, he was in a quandary about his future. For a short time he tried being a reporter. He worked for the Hearst International News Service, covering the charter meeting of the United Nations and the English elections of 1946. However, he was not happy. He wanted to be involved in the action, not just reporting on it.

In the spring of 1946, he made up his mind. Politics was what he wanted. He would run for Representative from the 11th district of Massachusetts to Congress. He campaigned with vigor, determination, and spirit. That fall he was elected, and in January 1947 he took his seat in the House of Representatives.

In 1952, after three terms in the House, he announced that he would run for the United States Senate. All odds were against his winning. He would be running against Henry Cabot Lodge, who had held the Senate seat since 1936.

But the odds-makers did not figure on the Kennedy will to win. John F. Kennedy and his family threw themselves into the campaign with all the enthusiasm, efficiency, and effectiveness that was customary of the Kennedys. In the same election in which Republican Dwight D. Eisenhower defeated Democrat Adlai E. Stevenson for the Presidency by an immense majority, Democrat John F. Kennedy defeated Republican Henry Cabot Lodge for the Senate seat from Massachusetts. He assumed his seat on January 3, 1953.

Just before Jack Kennedy began campaigning for Senator, he had met Jacqueline Lee Bouvier, who was working as the Inquiring Camera Girl on the *Washington Times Herald*.

Jacqueline had spent her childhood on Long Island and in New York City. Possessed of an unusual amount of grace, beauty and intelligence, she had also, under the competent direction of her mother, become an outstanding horsewoman. This combination of charm, beauty, and a facility in the out-of-doors appealed to Jack Kennedy. He began seeing her—off and on—for he was off campaigning and she was out of the country for a time.

The courtship was spasmodic. Both were busy. Life in the Senate was hectic for a young senator, and Kennedy was anxious to do a good job. Nevertheless, the two eventually became engaged and on September 12, 1953, Jacqueline Lee Bouvier and John Fitzgerald Kennedy were married in St. Mary's Church, Newport, Rhode Island.

Nineteen-fifty-four was a busy year in the Senate. And young Senator Kennedy, newly married and almost newly elected, was busier than most. Under pressure, his old back injury began to trouble him again. But at first he chose to ignore it. Not until he was forced to walk with crutches did he give in. Then on October 21, 1954, doctors at the Hospital for Special Surgery in New York City attempted a spinal operation to help him. It failed, and his convalescence was painful, long and unsatisfactory. In February 1955, another operation was attempted, this one somewhat more successful. Not until late in the year, however, after some special treatments, did he begin to get real relief from pain. It was while he was recuperating from his operations that he wrote *Profiles in Courage*, which won the Pulitzer Prize for biography in 1957.

Back in the Senate, he threw himself into the work to be done. In fact, he had never really left it, for all during his illness, his correspondence and what work he could do had followed him. In 1956, he campaigned for the vice-presidential nomination and narrowly missed receiving it. Although he was not a candidate, he was better known after the convention and the elections of that year than he had been before. People were beginning to watch what he was doing, and he was careful to do the things that clearly expressed the kind of person he was.

The main excitement in 1957 was completely personal. On November 27, Caroline Bouvier Kennedy was born in New York City. It was the first child for the Senator and his wife.

In 1958, it became very clear that John Kennedy was a popular man in Massachusetts. He was re-elected to his Senate seat by the greatest margin the people of Massachusetts had ever given a candidate. What was equally important was the fact that he had become known throughout the nation. It was obvious that he had strong support if he wanted to run for the Presidency. In fact, it became increasingly apparent that if he ever intended to run, he would be wise to consider doing so in 1960. The tide was running, partly by chance and partly by plan, in his direction.

By late 1959, John Kennedy had made up his mind. The Presidency offered a challenge he could not ignore. He began at once to campaign in earnest for the Democratic nomination. His brother, Robert, became his campaign manager, and as usual, the whole family and large numbers of friends went to work, too. On July 13, 1960, the Democratic National Convention nominated John Fitzgerald Kennedy to be its candidate for President.

Again the Kennedy system and the Kennedy ability went to work. The campaign against Richard Nixon was well organized, exciting, and effective. Every possible avenue to success was tried. The hours were long, and the tensions and pressures great, but Kennedy and his followers seemed to mass produce energy. There was time for the grand gestures, the large speeches, careful preparation for the TV debates with Nixon, and all the usual campaign clutter. But there was also time for the small human gestures that made individuals feel he was their candidate.

On November 8, 1960, John F. Kennedy was elected President of the United States. He was the youngest man and the first Roman Catholic to hold the office.

Seventeen days after the election, the Kennedy's second child, John F. Kennedy Jr. was born. He was baptized in the chapel at Georgetown Hospital, and a few days later the President-elect's family flew to Florida for the Christmas holiday at Joseph Kennedy's Palm Beach home. It seemed like a good place to rest, and a good place to plan and organize the new administration.

In Washington, D. C., on January 20, 1961, a bitter cold day, John F. Kennedy took the oath of office. Coatless in the wind, he delivered his inaugural address. He called for service to country and for sacrifice to attain the goals he felt would give America a future worthy of her past.

Among other things, his program called for medical care for the aged, federal aid to education, and major legislation to insure equal rights for all people in the United States regardless of race, economic status or place of residence.

These plans and others, for the United States at home and abroad, were known collectively as the "New Frontier." Not all of them were accepted as soon or as fully as Kennedy wanted them to be. There were disappointments and there were mistakes in both national and international matters. Yet many good ideas not immediately carried out had been injected into people's thinking and a constant subtle bolstering kept them alive and working until they were eventually acted upon.

It was a time of trouble and change, a time of growth throughout the world. It was a time that needed leadership, and John Kennedy was willing to try to give it. One of his major proposals for the world at large was the Peace Corps. This volunteer service for people of all ages who wanted to help other countries began shortly after he took office. It brought America and American skills to problems of every sort in hundreds of remote places where Americans had never been seen before.

Kennedy himself went abroad. He and Mrs. Kennedy spent time in France, where he talked with President de Gaulle about mutual problems.

There were many dealings with Russia. In 1962, Kennedy demanded that the U.S.S.R. withdraw the offensive weapons it had placed in Cuba, and the Soviets had to comply with the request. Yet he was able to meet on quite friendly terms with Chairman Khrushchev in Vienna. And out of this meeting there came, eventually, a limited nuclear test ban treaty.

On a visit to Mexico and South America he publicized his Alliance for Progress
program, designed to help the Latin American people develop a more prosperous
economy and a more equitable society.

Yet, wherever he went, Hyannis Port was home to Jack Kennedy. There he went to be with his family and friends and to relax by the sea. Children of all kinds—his son, his daughter, his nieces, his nephews and their friends—swarmed about the President, and he loved it. He organized relay races and swimming competitions for them and took them for rides on an electric golf cart to get candy at the nearby country store. These few carefree days gave him the moments of change he needed to approach the problems of the Presidency with a fresh mind and a new outlook. This, most of all, was what he wanted to do, and what he did.

On November 22, 1963, in Dallas, Texas, President John F. Kennedy was assassinated. He was buried at Arlington National Cemetery on November 25, 1963.

For days, for weeks, for months, for years, the people of the United States and of the world mourned the loss of a President and of a great world leader. He had been in office less than three years; he had not achieved all he had set out to do. But he had brought a new focus to old problems and a fresh vision for the future. The world was different, and always will be different, because he lived.